ICELAND

...in Pictures

Visual Geography Series®

ICELAND

...in Pictures

Prepared by
Geography Department

Lerner Publications Company
Minneapolis

Photo © Mats Wibe Lund

Farmers use dogs and horses to round up a herd of sheep in northern Iceland.

This book is an all-new edition of the Visual Geography Series. Previous editions were published by Sterling Publishing Company, New York City. The text, set in 10/12 Century Textbook, is fully revised and updated, and new photographs, maps, charts, and captions have been added.

LIBRARY OF CONGRESS CATALOGING-IN-PUBLICATION DATA

Iceland in pictures / prepared by Geography Department, Lerner Publications Company.
　　p. cm. – (Visual geography series)
　　Rev. ed. of: Iceland in pictures / prepared by John B. Burks, Jr.
　　Includes index.
　　Summary: An introduction to the geography, history, government, people, and economy of Europe's farthest outpost.
　　ISBN 0-8225-1892-9 (lib. bdg.)
　　1. Iceland. [1. Iceland.]　I. Burks, John B., 1942– Iceland in pictures. II. Lerner Publications Company. Geography Dept.　III. Series: Visual geography series (Minneapolis, Minn.)
DL315.I24　　1991
949.12—dc20
　　　　　　　　　　　　　　　　90-48206

International Standard Book Number: 0-8225-1892-9
Library of Congress Catalog Card Number: 90-48206

VISUAL GEOGRAPHY SERIES®

Publisher
Harry Jonas Lerner
Associate Publisher
Nancy M. Campbell
Senior Editor
Mary M. Rodgers
Editors
Gretchen Bratvold
Dan Filbin
Photo Researcher
Kerstin Coyle
Editorial/Photo Assistant
Marybeth Campbell
Consultants/Contributors
John G. Rice
Phyllis Schuster
Sandra K. Davis
Designer
Jim Simondet
Cartographer
Carol F. Barrett
Indexers
Kristin I. Spangard
Sylvia Timian
Production Manager
Gary J. Hansen

Independent Picture Service

Boats filled with freshly caught herring wait to be unloaded at an Icelandic port.

Acknowledgments

Title page photo © 1991 Mats Wibe Lund.

Elevation contours adapted from *The Times Atlas of the World*, second comprehensive edition (New York: Times Books, 1985).

2 3 4 5 6 7 8 9 10 – JR – 04 03 02 01 00 99 98 97 96

Courtesy of John Rice

Lava covered the houses on Heimaey, an island off the coast of southern Iceland, after a volcano erupted for six months in 1973. All the residents of this town were evacuated before the disaster. The lava also threatened to block Heimaey's harbor, but the eruption stopped before the docks were engulfed. Instead, the hardened lava added nearly a square mile of land to the island.

Contents

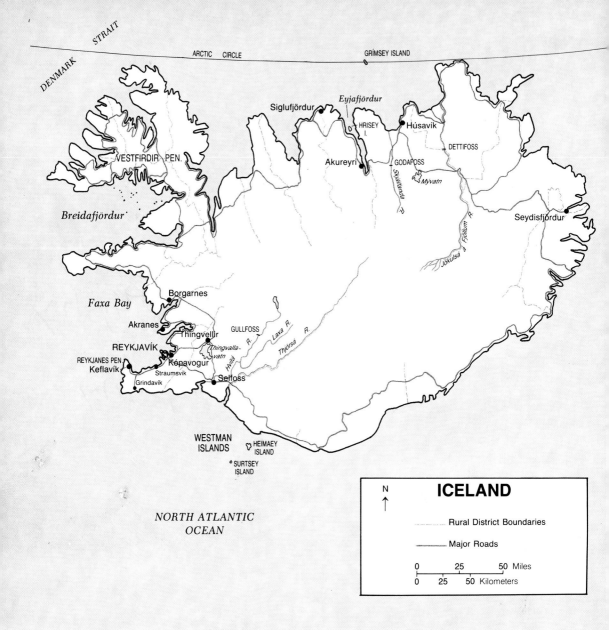

STRAIT

DENMARK

ARCTIC CIRCLE

GRÍMSEY ISLAND

Eyjafjördur

Siglufjördur

HRÍSEY I.

Húsavík

DETTIFOSS

VESTFIRDIR PEN.

Akureyri

GODAFOSS

Myvatn

Skjálfanda R.

Breidafjördur

Seydisfjördur

Jökulsá á Fjöllum R.

Faxa Bay

Borgarnes

Akranes

Thingvellir

GULLFOSS

Thingvalla-vatn

Hvítá R.

Laxa R.

Thjórsá R.

REYKJAVÍK

REYKJANES PEN.

Kópavogur

Straumsvík

Keflavík

Grindavík

Selfoss

WESTMAN ISLANDS

HEIMAEY ISLAND

SURTSEY ISLAND

NORTH ATLANTIC OCEAN

N

ICELAND

.... Rural District Boundaries

———— Major Roads

0   25   50 Miles

0   25   50 Kilometers

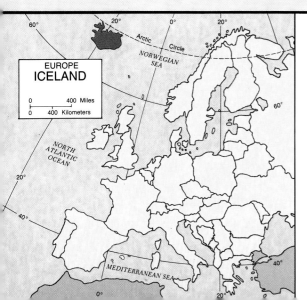

60°

20°

0°

20°

Arctic Circle

NORWEGIAN SEA

EUROPE
ICELAND

0   400 Miles

0   400 Kilometers

60°

NORTH ATLANTIC OCEAN

20°

40°

MEDITERRANEAN SEA

40°

0°

20°

Many people in Reykjavík, the capital of Iceland, paint their homes bright colors. Dominating the city's skyline is Hallgrim's Church, in front of which is a statue of Leif Eriksson. This early explorer, who was born in Iceland in the tenth century A.D., left the island on expeditions to North America.

Introduction

The Republic of Iceland is an independent island nation that sits in the middle of the North Atlantic Ocean close to the Arctic Circle. About four-fifths of the country is uninhabitable, not because of cold weather, but because the land cannot support vegetation. The climate, in fact, is quite bearable most of the time. On the interior of the island—with its lava deserts, rocky plateaus, mountains, and ice fields—little if any vegetation grows.

Iceland has a well-documented history dating from A.D. 874, when according to tradition the first permanent settlers arrived. Most of these pioneers emigrated from western Norway, but some came

Formed millions of years ago by volcanic eruptions, Iceland still experiences these powerful explosions. A long plume of smoke accompanied the lava that flowed from Hekla Volcano in 1947.

from Sweden, Denmark, and the British Isles. Having learned of the island from explorers, the newcomers chose it as a place to build their own society. The harsh environment tested their strength and commitment. Survival in Iceland involved prolonged struggles against natural disasters.

In 930 the settlers established the Althing, a representative government that wrote a code of laws. The annual meeting of this governmental assembly helped Icelanders to make important decisions. It also brought families together from their isolated farms and gave people a chance to share folktales and legends—which have

Icelandic ponies are a common form of overland transportation on the rugged island.

The flat plain at Thingvellir is the site of Iceland's earliest representative assembly, which began meeting in A.D. 930. One of the assembly's first laws prohibited any more horses from entering the country. In time, these limits protected the purity of Icelandic breeds.

Independent Picture Service

remained important parts of Icelandic culture.

By the thirteenth century, Icelanders had used up the island's timber, preventing them from building any more boats. The people also had worn out Iceland's grazing lands. Faced with these hardships, the people turned to Norway for help, offering their loyalty to the Norwegian king. When Norway came under Danish rule in 1380, so did Iceland. The island remained under Denmark's control until the twentieth century.

By 1900 Iceland's fishing industry had grown and had fostered the country's economic development. Icelanders built small factories to process the fish and laid roads to move goods. The pace of modernization sped up after 1950, when foreign demand for Iceland's fish increased.

The country used its new income to develop an extensive welfare system that cares for the nation's citizens from birth to old age. But this achievement is now endangered by a decline in national earnings from fishing and related businesses.

Iceland has clashed, sometimes violently, with northern European countries over the right to fish in the waters of the North Atlantic. To lessen its dependence on fishing, Iceland is trying to develop new manufacturing industries. The country also has a valuable future export in the form of geothermal energy. The people of Iceland have survived isolation, scarce resources, and a harsh climate. They are also proud to have the Althing, the world's oldest representative assembly. In the 1990s, their leaders must prepare them to meet economic competition from the lands of their ancestors in Europe.

Photo © Mats Wibe Lund

Since the early 1900s, fishing has been Iceland's main source of income. Here, workers salt herring at Siglufjördur, a port in the northern part of the country.

9

Water cascades down a jagged hillside and into a small stream in southern Iceland. Although vegetation is sparse, the area's terrain has its own harsh beauty.

1) The Land

Although considered part of Europe, Iceland is a long way from any continent. The nearest landmass is Greenland, which lies 180 miles to the northwest across the Denmark Strait. Iceland's closest European neighbor is Norway, which sits 645 miles to the east on the Scandinavian Peninsula.

Iceland is oval in shape, except for the jagged Vestfirdir Peninsula in the northwest. Covering a land area of 39,756 square miles, the country is about the size of the state of Kentucky. The greatest distance from east to west is 300 miles, and Iceland stretches for about 190 miles from north to south. The coastline, including fjords and other narrow sea inlets, is about 3,700 miles long.

Many small islands lie near the coast of the main island. The largest inhabited ones are Heimaey to the south, Hrisey to the north, and Grímsey on the Arctic Circle. These islands are sparsely populated. No one lives on the many tiny isles that lie in Breidafjördur (Broad Fjord), which is south of the Vestfirdir Peninsula.

Topography

Volcanic eruptions and lava flows formed Iceland millions of years ago. Yet it is a young country geologically and is still affected by movements deep within the earth.

Most of the interior is made up of an elevated plateau that lies 1,500 to 2,000 feet above sea level. Running north to south near the island's center, volcanic mountains and high tablelands rise above

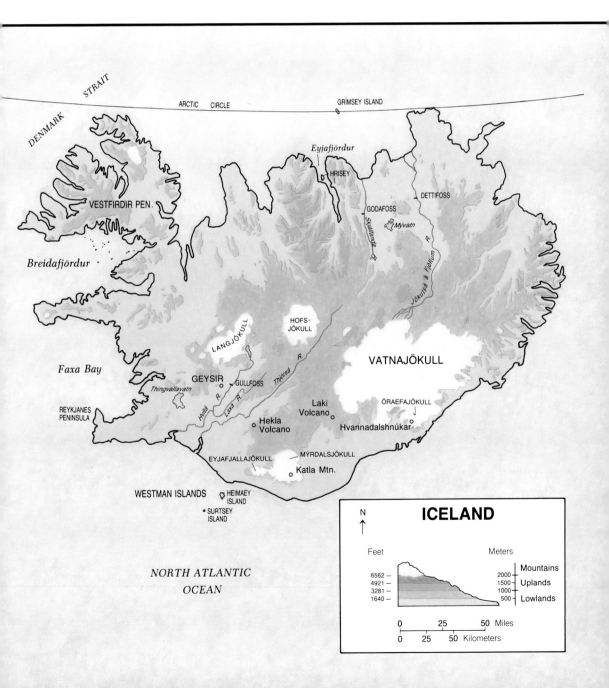

the plateau. This part of Iceland sits on top of the Mid-Atlantic Ridge, an underwater mountain chain. The sides, or plates, that form the ridge are slowly separating a few inches each year. This slight movement is enough to trigger powerful volcanic upheavals about once every five years.

The highest point in Iceland is Hvannadalshnúkar, a 6,952-foot peak in the Öraefajökull, a large glacier in southeastern Iceland. (In Icelandic, *jökull* means "glacier.") Öraefajökull sits next to Vatnajökull, an even bigger ice mass in the southeast.

A large, fertile plain of grasslands lies along the southwestern coast, Iceland's lowest-lying region. Grassy lowlands also extend inward from the fjords that cut into the western, northern, and eastern coasts. The deep inlets have created steep valleys, whose walls reveal successive layers of lava deposited by many volcanic eruptions.

A section of the Mid-Atlantic Ridge creates irregular formations near Thingvellir.

Courtesy of Steve Feinstein

In southwestern Iceland, snow-dusted mountains rise above the rocky, barren landscape.

Photo by John R. Day

In 1963 undersea volcanic explosions off Iceland's southern coast began to spew lava, which then cooled and hardened on the seabed. Over time, the eruptions deposited enough material to break the water's surface, creating Surtsey Island, which is now a nature reserve.

Volcanoes and Thermal Features

One of the most active volcanic areas on earth, Iceland has seen the birth of about 200 volcanoes in the last 10,000 years. More than 150 eruptions from at least 30 volcanoes have occurred since the country was settled in the ninth century.

The most common type of volcanic activity in Iceland is a fissure eruption. It happens when hot vapors and liquids building underground break through a long crack in the earth's crust. In 1783, for example, a fissure eruption spewed lava, gas, and ashes from Laki Volcano. Laki's lava flow—the biggest in recorded history—covered an area of 218 square miles. The lava destroyed many farms. Gases and ashes caused even greater destruction than the lava did. Spreading through the air over the whole country, these pollutants poisoned Iceland's grasslands, causing a food shortage that killed thousands of people and animals.

A hot column of lava shoots straight upward during a volcanic blast.

Hekla Volcano has destroyed vast areas since Iceland was settled. One eruption that began in March 1947 lasted 13 months, and the lava flow covered 25 square miles. Underwater eruptions near Iceland's coast have also occurred frequently. One such explosion created the island of Surtsey in 1963.

The presence of large glaciers in volcanic areas creates the additional hazards of sudden ice melts and flash floods in Iceland. The country suffered severe damage, for example, when Katla Mountain—hidden beneath Mýrdalsjökull—erupted in 1918. Katla's heat and hot lava rapidly melted part of the glacier, sending cascades of water through the surrounding countryside.

Iceland's volcanic activity also appears in less destructive ways, including geysers, hot springs, and steam vents. The country's Geysir, for example, spouts a column of boiling water and steam 180 feet into the air. (The word *geyser* comes from Iceland's Geysir.)

Courtesy of Iceland Tourist Board

Iceland's famous Geysir, from which the English word *geyser* comes, sends up a tower of steam at regular intervals.

Photo by John R. Day

Hot springs—a relatively safe thermal feature in Iceland—exist throughout the island.

Huge Vatnajökull dominates the landscape of southeastern Iceland. This glacier, or slow-moving mass of ice, covers an area half as large as the state of New Jersey.

The regions of thermal activity in Iceland are called *solfataras.* Some solfataras contain workable deposits of sulfur, one of the country's few mineral resources. The lava also heats underground water, which pipes bring to homes and businesses.

Glaciers, Rivers, and Lakes

Glaciers cover about 12 percent of Iceland's surface. They range in size from small, circular ice fields to large caps on mountains. The largest ice cap is Vatnajökull, which covers about 3,140 square miles. Northwest of Vatnajökull is Hofsjökull, which occupies 375 square miles. To the west of Hofsjökull is Langjökull, which has about 390 square miles of surface area.

Two smaller glaciers, Mýrdalsjökull and Eyjafjallajökull, sit south of Vatnajökull.

Fed by heavy rainfall, many swift rivers cut through Iceland. Strong currents, however, prevent boats from using these waterways. Running across the southern part of the country for more than 140 miles is the Thjórsá, the island's longest river. It begins in the central highlands northeast of Hofsjökull and flows southwest through the southern lowlands. Fifteen miles west of the Thjórsá is the Hvítá River, which travels southwest for about 80 miles to reach the Atlantic Ocean.

Iceland harnesses some of its rivers to produce hydroelectricity. The steep courses of other rivers create many high, impressive waterfalls, including Gullfoss

15

The broad cascades of Godafoss (meaning "Waterfall of the Gods") lie in northern Iceland on the Skjálfanda River.

Independent Picture Service

A shallow lake in northeastern Iceland, Mývatn is known for its wildlife, its scenery, and its unusual volcanic formations.

Courtesy of John Rice

on the Hvítá. Two other powerful falls—Godafoss and Dettifoss—are in northern Iceland. Godafoss lies along the Skjálfanda River, and Dettifoss is on Jökulsá á Fjöllum, which flows out of Vatnajökull.

Iceland has many lakes, but most are small. Among the largest are Thingvallavatn in the southwest and Mývatn in the north. (In Icelandic, *vatn* means "lake.") Thingvallavatn covers 32 square miles and is surrounded by flat, open plains that lead to low mountain ridges. Situated east of the town of Akureyri in northern Iceland

is Mývatn. The area surrounding this lake abounds in hot springs, craters, and sulfur pits. From the clear waters of Mývatn rise unusual lava formations that resemble giant abstract sculptures. A famous bird sanctuary near the lake attracts dedicated bird-watchers from around the world.

Climate

Despite its forbidding name and northern location, Iceland has a temperate climate. The warm waters of the Gulf Stream Current, which lap against all but Iceland's northern coast, make summers mild and winters cool but not unbearably cold. The ocean is colder in the north, where the Polar Current flows. In Reykjavík, the capital of Iceland, the average temperature is 52° F in July and 31° F in January. Average readings in northern Iceland are a little lower.

Probably the harshest aspects of Iceland's climate are the strong winds—which are constant in coastal regions—and the unpredictable weather. In the north, snowstorms have occurred in July. Rainfall varies greatly from region to region, but it is heaviest throughout the country in the winter. The south and southeast are the wettest regions. The southern coast receives about 82 inches of rain each year. Twice that amount falls on the southern slopes of the region's glaciers.

Situated south of the Arctic Circle, Iceland is one of the Lands of the Midnight Sun. In summer the sky never darkens completely, and even in late spring, twilights are long. From mid-November through January, on the other hand, Icelanders enjoy natural light only from about 1 P.M. to 3 P.M. When winter arrives, the colored arches of the *aurora borealis,* or northern lights, often play across the sky.

Flora

Iceland contains very few wooded areas. Many centuries ago, settlers cleared the birch and ash forests that grew in coastal regions. The largest birch woods that still stand are near Akureyri in the north and in eastern Iceland. Some rowan and aspen trees also exist in Iceland. The government protects the remaining woodlands and is

Strong winds push back young Icelanders standing at the edge of an inactive volcano on the Westman Islands.

is common throughout the country. Polar bears occasionally arrive on drifting ice masses, but these animals do not reproduce on the island. Many mink—which breeders brought to Iceland around 1930 for their fur—have escaped from farms and live in the wild. Reindeer, originally imported from Norway in the eighteenth century, roam in small herds over the island's northeastern highlands.

Icelandic ponies are descended from horses that early settlers brought to the island. Until the twentieth century, these small, surefooted horses were the nation's primary means of overland transportation. Breeding the horses over many generations has resulted in a very pure strain that the country carefully protects. No horses can be brought into Iceland, and if an Icelandic horse is taken overseas it cannot be brought back.

Courtesy of Leonard Soroka

Moss-covered rocks and white wildflowers add color to the country's bleak interior lava fields.

reforesting some areas with fast-growing evergreens.

About one-fourth of Iceland is covered with grass, which flourishes in the fertile valleys of the fjords and in the coastal lowlands. Mosses and lichens grow on the lower lava fields in the country's interior. Clinging to rocks and lava formations, these soft, green plants provide striking color in an otherwise drab landscape.

Low shrubs—such as heather (an evergreen with purple flowers) and dwarf willow—thrive in parts of the country that can support complex vegetation. Altogether, about 500 species of plants, many of which bloom or bear fruit, have adapted to Iceland's climate.

Fauna

Iceland has few wild animals. The only native land mammal is the arctic fox, which

Courtesy of Leonard Soroka

Clusters of lupines bloom in a garden in Húsavík, a town in northeastern Iceland.

Icelandic ponies are short and have tremendous strength. Most members of this sturdy breed, which is protected by law, have patient, quiet, and dependable natures. These ponies are easy to train and can take their riders almost anywhere on the rugged island.

Wind, snow, and sea have gouged holes in a cliff on the Westman Islands, where several kinds of birds find nesting places.

A group of puffins uses a rocky perch as a take-off and landing spot.

Independent Picture Service

More than 240 kinds of birds spend at least part of the year in Iceland. Seabirds, waterfowl, and wading birds are the most plentiful types. Puffins, kittiwakes, guillemots, gannets, and skuas lay their eggs in coastal rock cliffs. Many ptarmigan migrate to Iceland during the winter months, and hunters shoot them for food.

Various ducks, geese, and swans live in Iceland in the summer. Eider ducks are very common. Some Icelandic farmers earn money by hunting the ducks for their downy feathers, which are used to stuff pillows and quilts. Two birds of prey—the gyrfalcon and the eagle—have become rare and are now protected by law.

The North Atlantic waters surrounding Iceland are home to many species of fish, which breed in offshore beds. The most important commercial varieties of fish are cod, herring, haddock, ocean perch, halibut, and plaice. Although overfishing has seriously depleted other fish stocks, salmon are still plentiful. Most of the country's rivers and lakes are well stocked with trout. Many seals and some whales inhabit coastal waters.

Cities and Towns

More than half of Iceland's 300,000 citizens live in the Reykjavík metropolitan area, which includes the residential suburb of Kópavogur (population 17,000). Within the city itself—the world's northernmost capital—about 102,000 people make their homes. The next largest population center in Iceland is Akureyri, which lies at the midpoint along the northern coast. Small towns and villages, most of them clustered in the east and southwest, dot Iceland's coasts.

Photo © Mats Wibe Lund

Salmon are common in the country's fresh waters. Although several kinds of salmon exist, Iceland's are of the Atlantic type. Born in freshwater streams, Atlantic salmon spend part of their lives in salt water.

20

The town of Akureyri is northern Iceland's industrial hub. It also contains a botanical garden and museums that commemorate famous Icelandic poets.

REYKJAVIK

The economic, political, and cultural center of Iceland, Reykjavík (population 102,000) sits on a low peninsula that extends westward into Faxa Bay in southwestern Iceland. The capital's name means "smoky bay," which refers to the clouds of steam that billow forth from hot springs in the area. A small settlement for several hundred years, Reykjavík did not emerge as a town until the end of the eighteenth century, when about 300 Icelanders made the site their home. By 1910, after the development of fishing and of food-processing industries, Reykjavík had a population of 11,600.

The oldest parts of Reykjavík are the port area and the town's center. The sod-and-timber houses that Icelanders built before the twentieth century have all disappeared, and houses in the city are now made of concrete. Most of Iceland's museums and other cultural institutions are located in Reykjavík, which also is home to the country's only university.

Reykjavík is one of the few metropolitan areas in the world with no air pollution problems. The city's hot underground water provides clean energy to heat almost all the homes and businesses in the capital.

AKUREYRI

With about 15,000 citizens, Akureyri is on a fine natural harbor 35 miles up the Eyjafjördur, the longest fjord in Iceland. South of the town, a long narrow valley of fertile farmland cuts deep into the high, surrounding mountains. Akureyri is an old community mentioned in records that date from the 1400s, when the port settlement was a trading post.

Unlike most coastal communities in Iceland, Akureyri has a variety of industries, including a shoe factory, a tannery, and a wool-processing plant. Its port facilities, the surrounding farmland, and the productive fishing grounds in the Eyjafjördur have also been important to the city's economy.

OTHER TOWNS

About 30 miles southwest of Reykjavík is the town of Keflavík (population 7,500), located on the northern coast of the Reykjanes Peninsula. Cr ated by volcanic eruptions, the region still has active hot springs. Keflavík is also the site of an international military air base. Many Icelanders object to the installation, because they believe it makes their country a wartime target. Other citizens say that

Courtesy of Leonard Soroka

With a fine natural harbor, Reykjavík was a sensible choice for the nation's capital. Most of its houses get their hot water from pipelines that tap heated groundwater.

Keflavík's economy benefits from the air base, which provides many jobs.

Akranes (population 5,200), 20 miles north of Reykjavík across Faxa Bay, is a leading fishing port and contains the country's only cement plant. To the north of Akranes lies Borgarnes (population 1,400), the commercial center of the country's western agricultural district. The most important town on the fertile southern plain is Selfoss (population 4,050), which has Iceland's largest dairy industry.

Courtesy of USAF/Photo by Master Sergeant Michael E. Daniels

Keflavík sits on a peninsula in southwestern Iceland. Its international airport has commercial services for travelers and military facilities for U.S. fighter planes.

22

A stained-glass window depicts the arrival of some of Iceland's immigrants. Sailing from northwestern Europe in the ninth century A.D., the first pioneers imported animals, and later settlers brought the Christian religion to the island.

2) History and Government

As early as the fourth century B.C., navigators from southern Europe knew of the existence of Iceland. No traces of actual landings from this period have been found, however. Archaeologists think that a group of Celtic people from northern Europe may have lived in Iceland as early as A.D. 680.

No evidence exists that humans inhabited Iceland before the Europeans came.

The first records of settlement in Iceland date from about A.D. 800, when Irish monks built dwellings on the island. Little is known about these monks, who probably left Iceland during the 800s, when

23

adventurers from Norway and Sweden came to the island. These adventurers —called Vikings—continued their explorations westward into North America.

After hearing about Iceland from returning voyagers, a group of Norwegian Vikings decided to settle there. After spending two harsh winters on the island and seeing their cattle die, the members of this expedition abandoned their plan and returned to Norway. They gave the name Iceland to the land that had been so cold and severe.

Settlement

The first permanent inhabitants of Iceland arrived in A.D. 874. According to tradition, in that year the Viking leader Ingólfur Arnarson sailed to the island from western Norway with his family and servants. Legends say that Ingólfur, upon sighting

Independent Picture Service

In the A.D. 800s, Norwegian adventurers called Vikings journeyed to Iceland. Their swift boats were often decorated with fierce-looking, intricately carved animal heads.

land, followed a Viking custom. He threw into the sea his sacred pillars—symbolic columns that Viking leaders kept in their homes. The sea carried the pillars to a low peninsula on the southwestern coast of the island, and there Ingólfur established a farm. The site is now Reykjavík.

In the 60 years that followed, almost all of Iceland's pioneering settlers arrived. The largest number came from western Norway. Their journey normally took about seven days in the light, swift longboats that the Vikings used. Under the most favorable weather conditions, the trip could be completed in just four days.

Norwegians probably moved to Iceland to escape the rule of King Harald Fairhair, who was unifying Norway in the late ninth century. The king attempted to establish authority over less powerful leaders in his country, some of whom left rather than submit to his control. At the same time, a small number of Danes and Swedes came to Iceland as well. But most of the Icelandic pioneers who did not originate in Norway were Celts from Ireland and Scotland. The Norwegians usually brought these Celts to Iceland as wives or as slaves (called thralls).

The earliest arrivals claimed large tracts of coastal land and divided the property among their immediate families, relatives, and friends. They established separate, largely self-sufficient farming communities. Later settlers had to survive on the smaller plots of land that were left. By A.D. 930, people had claimed almost all inhabitable areas around the coast of Iceland. Then, as now, the interior of the island was uninhabitable.

The Althing and the Republic

People in the various parts of Iceland had strong leaders—called *godar*—to settle disputes between neighbors and to make important decisions. In some places, local assemblies met to choose and advise the godar.

A national park and scattered farm buildings now occupy Thingvellir, the valley where Iceland's first parliament – the Althing – began to meet in A.D. 930.

Communication among districts was difficult throughout Iceland. Roads did not exist, and travel was by boat, on foot, or on horseback. Yet, as the population grew, contact and cooperation became necessary. The settlers also wanted a system of laws and courts that would apply to every region.

In A.D. 930, the godar met near Reykjavík to establish a national government. These leaders formed the Althing, or national parliament, and founded the Icelandic republic. The godar, together with the lawspeaker of the assembly, formed the lawmaking branch of the Althing. The lawspeaker could recite all the laws from memory.

The godar also had religious duties. During the time when the Norse religion from Norway was followed, the godar maintained the places where people worshiped Norse gods. Later, after Christianity came to Iceland, the leaders chose Christian priests to serve the people.

The Althing moved to Thingvellir, a valley by Thingvallavatn, and met annually for two weeks. The event was important for social as well as political reasons. Entire families attended, and some came from remote areas. People used the opportunity to buy and sell goods and livestock, to arrange marriages, and to exchange news. Games, tournaments, fairs, and markets during the Althing gave Icelanders relief from their isolation.

One favorite activity at Thingvellir was storytelling—the reciting of folktales and poetry—which became the foundation of Iceland's cultural heritage. The annual event also allowed people to discuss law, government, and public affairs.

Conflicts and Changes

No single leader ran Iceland's government, and the system developed by the godar worked well for a few decades. The population lived by raising livestock, by

Much of what is known about Iceland's early history, as well as about some European events, comes from Icelandic sagas. These long, often heavily illustrated works describe heroes, heroines, and battles. Here, a page from an Icelandic manuscript depicts the killing of Olaf II, an eleventh-century king of Norway, during the Battle of Stiklestad in 1030.

fishing, and by hunting seals and waterfowl. Settlers built a large fleet of boats with timber from Iceland's forests. Although still small in size, Reykjavík became the political and commercial center of the island. In the summer, Icelanders crossed the Atlantic to sell textiles, wool, hides, gyrfalcons, and sulfur in Europe. They returned with grain, timber, tar, linen, and manufactured goods.

The Icelandic settlers practiced the Norse religion. They worshiped various gods, including the male deities Thor and Odin and the goddess Freya. By the end of the tenth century, however, a few Christian missionaries had come to Iceland from Germany. They introduced the one-god Roman Catholic faith that Norway had also adopted. Conflicts arose between followers of the new Christian religion and supporters of the old ways.

In A.D. 1000, to avoid civil war, the godar decided that Iceland must adopt Christianity. They also hoped their decision would persuade the Christian king of Norway, Olaf I Tryggvason, to release some Icelanders he was holding captive.

By 1100 Iceland had ended slavery, which had existed on the island since the first settlers came. In the same period, scholars adapted the Latin alphabet for use in the Icelandic language. At religious centers, priests taught some of the people to read and write.

In these early years, Icelanders worked hard to make their society self-sufficient. They spent their days farming, fishing, spinning, weaving, and boatbuilding. During the long, dark days of winter, family members listened to a storyteller while making nets, clothing, and other necessary items.

Icelandic society from 930 to 1030 is well known because of the events recorded in the sagas—the country's long, detailed literary works. Although the accounts are considered fictional, they are based on actual happenings. Icelanders retold the stories, passing them on to later generations. Educated Icelanders wrote down the sagas between 1120 and 1230.

The Republic's Decline

In the 1100s, the growing strength and wealth of the Roman Catholic Church in Iceland began to weaken the power of the godar in some districts of the country. The decline of those godar allowed a few others to expand their families' property and influence. Eventually, six strong families dominated Iceland.

After 1200, bloody struggles broke out between these families. Historians call this period the Sturlung age, after the Sturlung family, which attempted to gain political control. At the same time, Norway's religious leaders urged Icelanders to submit to the Norwegian king's authority.

During this unstable period, Icelanders faced increasingly difficult challenges. The earlier settlers had cut down most of the trees. As old ships fell apart, the people had no wood to build new ones. Much of the country's trade fell into the hands of Norwegian merchants. In addition, overgrazing by sheep had destroyed large areas of vegetation. As the climate began to cool, farmers found it more difficult to grow crops.

By 1220 King Haakon IV of Norway had taken advantage of the strife among

Life was not easy for Icelandic settlers. People usually lived in sod-and-timber houses built into hillsides. Furniture was simple and sturdy. Entire families might share only one room, where cooking, eating, sleeping, and fish drying took place.

Photo by Bettmann Archive

Queen Margrete of Denmark, who also ruled Iceland in the late 1300s, focused her attention on her larger holdings in Scandinavia (Norway, Denmark, and Sweden). As a result, Iceland made little progress during her reign, which ended in 1412.

From 1402 to 1404, the Black Death (a fatal disease spread by rats) reached Iceland from Europe. This plague killed two-thirds of the population. As the century passed, volcanic eruptions, floods, and earthquakes further damaged the country. The climate grew colder as a 400-year period called the Little Ice Age began. In the 1500s, farmers stopped growing grain because of the extremely cold weather. With no grain, the livestock that survived had to feed on grass.

Following the Black Death, the population of Europe increased as the survivors began to have large families. Demand grew for fish and for fish oil, which were inexpensive foods. English and German merchants came to Iceland throughout the fifteenth century seeking these products. The competition between the English and the Germans for Iceland's fish catch drove up the price and helped the Ice-

Iceland's warring families to assert his authority over the republic. Worn out by internal feuding, Icelanders pledged their loyalty to the Norwegian king between 1262 and 1264. Yet rule by Norway did not improve conditions in Iceland. Years of failed harvests brought increasing economic hardships. By the late 1300s, famine had caused deaths among the population and threatened Iceland's survival.

Danish Rule

When Haakon VI of Norway died in 1380, his wife, Margrete, who ruled Denmark, became the queen of Norway as well. Iceland, too, came under the Danish crown. After the Union of Kalmar—which united Denmark, Norway, and Sweden in 1397—lawmaking power in Iceland was shared jointly by the Icelandic Althing and the Danish monarch. Queen Margrete took little action to address the island's problems, however, and Icelandic economic affairs continued to worsen under Danish control.

Photo by Philadelphia Museum of Art,
SmithKline Beckman Corporation Fund

A woodcut portrays a patient suffering from the plague. This disease, sometimes called the Black Death because black spots of blood formed under the skin, killed two-thirds of Iceland's population in the early 1400s.

landers to survive. Danish rulers, however, wanted Denmark to have the exclusive right to trade with Iceland. Christian III, who became the Danish king in 1536, banned Iceland's trade with all non-Danish merchants.

Despite resistance from loyal Icelandic Catholics, Christian III also replaced the Roman Catholic faith with the Protestant Lutheran religion. Since the early 1300s, Iceland's Roman Catholic officials had been foreigners, and they had gradually acquired wealth and property. Christian III gained great riches when he took over the lands belonging to the Catholic monasteries and officials.

DENMARK TIGHTENS ITS CONTROL

In 1602 King Christian IV made even more income by gaining sole control over Iceland's trade. He allowed only specially licensed Danish merchants to engage in

Photo by Museum of National History, Frederiksborg

From 1588 to 1648, King Christian IV governed Denmark, which had authority over Iceland. He increased his royal income by taking complete control of Iceland's trade.

Courtesy of Library of Congress

An early drawing shows travelers trying to stay on their mounts during a trip across Iceland. The island's lack of roads hindered communication and development for many centuries.

commerce with Iceland. The king collected large sums for the licenses.

As a result, merchants shipped inferior goods and charged high prices for them, knowing Icelanders had no other source of supply. Items produced in Iceland, on the other hand, fetched only the very low prices that licensed merchants were willing to pay. Gradually, the Danish trade monopoly destroyed the wealth and influence of Iceland's ruling class and reduced the population to poverty.

In 1660 King Frederick III expanded his authority over his Danish subjects. By 1662 the king had imposed his power on Iceland's population as well. The Althing lost its lawmaking function, and its role as the final authority in legal disputes ended.

The 1700s

In the 1700s, a series of natural disasters threatened the existence of the Icelandic population. At the beginning of the cen-

Photo by Lee Meyer

Ice floes – large chunks of floating ice – often prevented boats from reaching Iceland's shores in the 1700s.

Volcanic eruptions caused additional difficulties in the eighteenth century. Laki Volcano exploded in 1783, killing most of the country's livestock and one-fifth of its people.

tury, the country had 50,000 people—half the number of inhabitants it had in 1100. A smallpox epidemic killed 15,000 people between 1707 and 1709. The population decreased further during famines in the middle of the 1700s, when winters were extremely cold. Large ice floes (floating chunks of ice) blocked coasts and caused several shipwrecks. When the ice floes melted in spring, they flooded many coastal settlements. Epidemics of disease severely reduced both the human and the animal populations.

One positive change did occur in the 1700s. In 1746 Denmark decreed that all parents must teach their children to read or must hire someone else to do so. Lutheran clergy throughout Iceland supervised reading programs, since most isolated farms had no access to schools. As a result of these programs, the Icelandic population had a very high rate of literacy by 1780.

Despite this sign of progress, the struggle for survival continued. One of the worst disasters in Iceland's history struck in 1783 and 1784, when Laki Volcano erupted in south central Iceland. The eruptions spread volcanic ash and poisonous gases throughout the island. The ash and gases ruined most of the farmland. The food shortage that resulted caused the deaths of 9,500 people—one-fifth of the population. The country also lost 77 percent of its horses, 53 percent of its cattle, and 82 percent of its sheep.

The disaster nearly exhausted Iceland's remaining sources of livelihood. In response, Denmark eased its trade monopoly and gave all subjects of the Danish king the right to trade with Icelanders. The king did not, however, yield any political control to local Icelandic leaders. The Althing, which had continued to judge some legal cases, assembled for the last time at Thingvellir in 1798.

Steps to Independence

In the early 1800s, General Napoleon Bonaparte of France attempted to conquer Europe but was defeated by an alliance of other European nations. The conflict caused upheaval and hardship throughout the continent. After his defeat, people in Europe sought changes in their political systems and improvements in living conditions. In 1830 the Danish king, yielding to the demands of his people, established an advisory assembly in Denmark.

Under the leadership of a young activist named Jón Sigurdsson, Icelanders also fought for more control over their own affairs. By 1840 Sigurdsson and his followers were demanding social, economic, and constitutional changes. They succeeded in restoring the Althing in 1843, but Denmark recognized it only as an advisory group.

In 1854 the Danish government permitted foreign countries to reestablish trade with Iceland. In 1874—the 1,000-year anniversary of the first permanent Icelandic settlement—Denmark granted Iceland a constitution and control of its own finances. As a result, the Althing gained more power and could pass laws with the consent of the Danish monarch. In 1882 the government established a national bank, which gave Icelanders better trading opportunities.

Yet life in Iceland was not easy in the 1870s and 1880s. No factories existed, and the country depended on agriculture for survival. Fishing helped to supply food, but this industry was not a source of income for most people. Farmers had formed cooperative agricultural societies, which improved farming methods. Nevertheless, poor weather and another serious volcanic upheaval offset the gains during these decades. Many discouraged farm families moved to Canada and the northern United States to survive.

The growth of Reykjavík dates from the 1800s, when the port's fishing industry began to attract many settlers.

Artwork by Laura Westlund

Officially adopted in 1915, Iceland's flag is similar to the emblem of Norway, which first colonized the island. Blue is Iceland's traditional color, standing for the sea and the sky. Red symbolizes the country's many active volcanoes, and white represents geysers and icebergs.

The Republic Returns

In the late 1800s, the local food problem slowly got better. Grasslands improved, creating more food for livestock. As the country raised more animals, it was also able to sustain a greater number of people. By 1890 Iceland's population numbered 70,900, and from that point it climbed rapidly. Death rates declined, and birthrates were high. Improved economic conditions slowed emigration, and eventually more people were moving into than leaving the country.

Despite these advances, farming remained difficult and risky. By the end of the 1800s, many owners of small farms—especially in the north—had abandoned their land and turned to fishing for their main source of income. New boats with enclosed decks replaced traditional rowboats. These improved vessels permitted crews to venture long distances from the coast and to catch more fish.

Conditions in Iceland continued to get better, and Denmark granted the country control over its internal affairs in 1904. In 1906 telegraphs linked Icelanders to other countries. Steam trawlers and motorboats made even longer fishing trips possible. Legislation passed in 1907 improved schooling, and four years later the University of Iceland opened.

Advances in transportation on the island also helped the country. Just before World War I (1914–1918), automobiles were introduced in Iceland, and they soon became the most important means of travel. In 1914 the new Iceland Steamship

33

Company began to handle much of the country's oceangoing trade.

In the same year, World War I broke out in Europe. Iceland did not take sides during this international conflict. Cut off from markets in Europe, the country began trading with North America. After the war ended, Iceland continued to prosper and resumed trade with Europe. On December 1, 1918, Denmark recognized Iceland's complete independence under the Treaty of Union, which either nation could end after 25 years. Denmark, however, remained partly responsible for Iceland's foreign affairs and defense.

Iceland's 1,000 years of isolation from European wars ended with the outbreak of World War II (1939–1945). After German troops occupied Denmark, the Danish government could no longer defend Iceland. Icelanders then took over responsibility for their own protection.

In May 1940, Great Britain, which was at war with Germany, sent troops to Iceland to prevent a German invasion. In June the Althing elected Icelander Sveinn Björnsson to temporarily govern the nation. In 1941, when Britain needed its soldiers in Iceland for duty in Europe, Iceland asked the United States for troops to replace the British forces.

The world war forced Iceland to take full control of its own affairs. The Icelandic people voted to formally declare their in-

Photo by Trustees of the Imperial War Museum, London

In 1940 British and Canadian troops *(above and right)* **were stationed in Iceland to protect it from possible German occupation during World War II (1939-1945).**

Photo by Trustees of the Imperial War Museum, London

On June 17, 1944, Sveinn Björnsson proclaimed Iceland a republic to crowds assembled at historic Thingvellir. From 1944 to 1952, Sveinn served as the first president of the new nation.

dependence from Denmark. The Althing ended the Treaty of Union with Denmark in 1944. At Thingvellir on June 17, 1944— the anniversary of Jón Sigurdsson's birth— the government proclaimed a new republic. Sveinn Björnsson was elected Iceland's first president.

The Postwar Period

World War II affected Iceland in several ways. The conflict stimulated the island's economy, because the warring nations needed Iceland's fish and other products.

As the war drew to a close, the United States asked to establish a permanent military base on Iceland. Sveinn and his cabinet did not want to grant the request, but the United States refused to pull its forces out of the country. In 1946 Iceland agreed to a compromise that allowed the United States to maintain control of the airport at Keflavík for a limited time.

After the war, Iceland strengthened its international ties by becoming a founding member of the United Nations. Although many of its people strongly objected, Iceland ended its policy of neutrality when it

Photo by John R. Day

Planes belonging to NATO—a defensive alliance of Western nations—stand ready for takeoff at Keflavík Airport. Iceland joined the alliance in 1951, and since then this air base has hosted troops and aircraft from the United States, another NATO member.

joined the North Atlantic Treaty Organization (NATO). The air base at Keflavík, with its U.S. forces, became a permanent installation of this defensive military alliance of Western nations.

Opponents of the NATO base said it interfered with Iceland's ability to govern itself and made the country a target for a nuclear attack. Supporters of the base, on the other hand, pointed out that it provided jobs and income for Icelanders.

THE COD WARS

Another international dispute occurred when Iceland sought to expand its claims to fishing rights in the North Atlantic Ocean. Immediately after World War II, the country declared the waters within 3 miles of its coasts as its exclusive fishing area. As more foreign trawlers fished nearby areas, Iceland extended the limit to 4 miles in 1952, to 12 miles in 1958, to 50 miles in 1972, and to 200 miles in 1975.

Each extension resulted in conflicts—the so-called "cod wars"—with Great Britain, whose fleet also fished in the North Atlantic. In response to Icelandic attacks against British trawlers, the British sent their navy into the area. Icelanders were strongly supportive of their government's efforts to protect the nation's main livelihood. At one point, Britain refused to purchase Iceland's fish products, and Iceland broke diplomatic relations with Britain.

A solution acceptable to both sides seemed unlikely until Iceland threatened to withdraw from NATO and to close the air base at Keflavík. Representatives of Iceland and Britain met with the head of NATO in 1976 to resolve the disagreement. They signed a pact that restricted British trawling within the 200-mile limit.

In the 1970s, during the cod wars between Iceland and Britain, an Icelandic demonstrator hurled a rock at the windows of the British embassy in Reykjavík.

Recent Developments

During these international events, Iceland's internal political situation remained stable. Icelanders freely expressed a variety of political views and formed many political parties. No single party or viewpoint dominated the government. Members of two or more different parties formed each cabinet, administering the government together under the leadership of a prime minister. The largest parties were the Independence, the Progressive, the People's Alliance, and the Social Democratic.

When the country's first president, Sveinn Björnsson, died in 1952, voters picked Ásgeir Ásgeirsson to succeed him. When Ásgeir retired in 1968, Kristján Eldjárn replaced him as president of Iceland. In

In the southwestern port of Grindavík, Icelandic fishermen work on shore before boats arrive with catches from the North Atlantic Ocean. By 1975 the nation had claimed exclusive fishing rights within 200 miles of its coasts.

Voters first elected Vigdís Finnbogadóttir president of Iceland in 1980 and again in 1984 and 1988. She remained in office even though many Icelandic cabinets formed and collapsed during the decade. A popular national figure, President Vigdís won 92 percent of the vote in the 1988 election. She won a fourth term in 1992 but retired in 1996.

Courtesy of Embassy of Iceland

June 1980, voters elected Vigdís Finnbogadóttir Iceland's first female president.

Vigdís's popularity increased the strength of a feminist political party called the Women's Alliance. In 1995 it received 5 percent of the votes and gained three legislative seats.

WHALING CONTROVERSY

For centuries, Iceland's fishermen have hunted whales for their flesh and oil, which are valuable exports. In the 1970s, environmental groups began to object to international whaling activities, including those of Iceland. By the 1980s, the International Whaling Commission, a group that protects whales from overhunting, had called for a temporary halt on the commercial killing of whales.

Iceland continued to hunt the animals, most of which belonged to the endangered fin and sei species. A controversy broke out in the mid-1980s, when some environmentalists tried to stop Iceland's whaling activities by sinking ships and destroying other equipment.

Iceland agreed to temporarily restrict whale killing to what is called research whaling. This practice takes whales for scientific study, and the whaling nation keeps most of the whale meat for its own markets. The Althing considered a proposal to ban whaling altogether, but it did not pass. Although whaling made up only a small part of Iceland's fishing activities, the government has strongly maintained the country's right to hunt whales.

ECONOMIC ISSUES

The government and people of Iceland have long recognized the need to create more export industries to broaden the country's fish-dependent economy. The opening of an aluminum smelter at Straumsvík in 1969 marked a step in that direction, and more industries followed. Many factories, however, remained tied to the all-important fishing industry.

Until the late 1980s, the country's economy prospered, even though prices for

In the 1970s and 1980s, Iceland weathered strong international protests over its whaling policy. The country gradually decreased the number of whales killed each year and in 1989 suspended its whaling program for two years. Nevertheless, Iceland withdrew from the International Whaling Commission, a whale conservation group, in 1992.

Icelanders shop at an open-air market in downtown Reykjavík. The nation's citizens buy many of their goods from foreign sources. As a resul , the cost of living can vary considerably. In 1988 and 1989, the government decreased the value of the national unit of money, the krona, three times. This devaluation meant that Icelanders paid more for goods in those years than they had in previous years.

goods rose sharply. At the end of the 1980s, however, Iceland's economy weakened. Prices rose, and unemployment increased. As a conservation measure, the country sharply reduced the number of fish it allowed Icelandic boats to catch. As a result, however, Iceland lost important export income.

In the 1990s, prime minister David Oddsson took measures to improve Iceland's economy. The government cut its budget deficit and loosened control of wages and prices. By the mid-1990s, the inflation rate had begun to go down. A growing economy allowed more Icelandic companies to hire workers, and unemployment fell. But Iceland still faces the problems posed by an economy dependent on fishing.

Government

Iceland's president, who is elected to a four-year term, is the head of state and has limited powers. The president helps to form a government after national elections take place and appoints the cabinet ministers, including the prime minister. This official is usually from the party that holds the most seats in the legislature.

The prime minister is the most powerful political figure in Iceland, and, with the assistance of the cabinet, carries out the country's laws. The prime minister and the cabinet must have the support of a majority in the Althing to remain in office. Cabinet members need not be elected members of the Althing.

The Althing, the legislative body, consists of 63 members, who serve four-year terms. Delegates vote on the budget and other financial bills in the unicameral (one-house) Althing. Bills are discussed three times before a vote is taken.

The judicial system consists of a supreme court composed of eight judges and a chief justice. Lower courts are run by district judges and magistrates. Special tribunals hear cases relating to the seas, to labor disputes, and to certain other matters. A judge, rather than a jury, hears criminal cases and may also call upon specialists to consider the case.

For administrative purposes, Iceland is divided into rural provinces, each headed by an officer appointed by the central government. In addition, there are incorporated towns that are headed by town councils. All citizens who are at least 18 years of age can vote.

The Althing meets in a brick building that faces a square in central Reykjavík. The parliament's 63 members debate laws and budgetary matters.

Photo © 1991 Mats Wibe Lund

Wearing traditional Icelandic costumes, folk dancers perform at National Day celebrations in Reykjavík. The festival, held annually on June 17, marks the anniversary of Iceland's full independence from Danish control.

3) The People

Most of Iceland's 300,000 inhabitants are descendants of the country's original settlers. They were mainly Norse people from Norway and Celtic folk from the British Isles. Icelanders take great pride in their ancestries and often can trace them back many generations. Very few immigrants of other ethnic backgrounds have moved to Iceland.

With an average of seven people per square mile, Iceland is sparsely populated. Since four-fifths of the country is uninhabited, however, the density is actually greater in cities and towns, where about 90 percent of the population live. Compared to other industrialized nations, the cost of living in Iceland is high. Nearly everything that people use must be imported, and most families need more than one income to support themselves.

Many young Icelandic couples do not marry until they can afford their own house or apartment. Until they are self-sufficient, couples live together with one set of parents, and many have children before marriage. Three-fourths of Iceland's firstborns have unmarried parents. Baptism of the first child often happens on the same day as the marriage of the parents.

Iceland's women have gained greater political influence since 1975. On one day in that year, the nation's women stopped working at jobs inside and outside their homes as a way of demonstrating their important role in the country's activities. In 1985 women again went on strike—to mark the tenth anniversary of the first strike. Even President Vigdís stayed home from work.

Health and Social Welfare

Iceland has one of the highest birthrates in western Europe and one of the highest life expectancies—79 years—in the world. These factors are causing the population to increase faster than in other European nations. If present trends continue, the population of Iceland will double in 68 years. This change could put more pressure on the country's limited land and food. In addition, jobs could become harder to find.

The director of public health oversees matters related to the population's health. Iceland's hospitals offer high-quality medical services, and governmental insurance plans cover costs for people who are ill or injured.

Iceland is a welfare state, meaning that the government provides for the well-being of its people. The country's social-security program makes sure that all citizens have an income. The program's benefits also include pensions for the retired and the disabled. The government makes payments to families with children under 18 and to orphans. Assistance to widows and to single mothers is also part of Iceland's welfare system.

Iceland's 1990 Budget

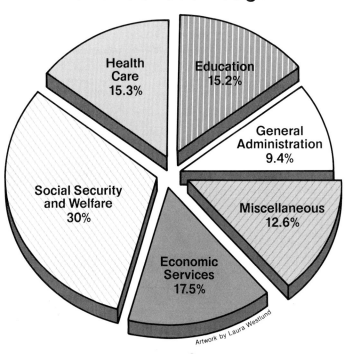

This pie chart shows the percentages of Iceland's budget that go to various national programs. Expenses for social programs take up the largest pieces of the pie. General administrative costs include law enforcement. Economic services cover government payments to farmers, fisheries, and industry.

Children practice kicking soccer balls in a playing field outside their school.

This comprehensive program is costly, and Icelanders pay high taxes to fund it. Iceland spends most of its tax income on social security, which takes about 30 percent of the national budget. Another large slice goes to farmers to help cover their costs in raising food. Education claims 12 percent of government spending.

Education

Since the late 1700s, Iceland has had a high literacy rate, but the country did not require all children to go to school until 1907. Most schools are state run and free. All Icelandic students study Danish and English as well as Icelandic. High-school students also study French, German, and Latin.

Beginning at age six, Icelandic children attend primary school for seven years and then go to lower secondary school for two years. They can then attend a middle school for one or two years, taking academic or vocational courses. Students who complete middle school usually enter a high school, where they can prepare for admission to a university.

A wrought-iron sculpture on the wall of a high school in Reykjavík shows the many technical trades that are taught at this vocational institution.

43

Students are normally 20 years old when they enter Iceland's largest institution of higher learning, the University of Iceland in Reykjavík. Founded in 1911 when three smaller colleges merged, the national university offers courses in medicine, law, economics, theology, engineering, and other subjects. The country also has specialized schools for career training in teaching, business, agriculture, and nautical science. For higher education in certain academic fields, Icelanders go to foreign, usually Scandinavian, universities.

Language

The Icelandic language belongs to the Scandinavian group, which is Germanic in origin. Written Icelandic has changed little over the centuries and closely resembles the language that the island's first Scandinavian settlers used. Icelandic children can read and understand the sagas in the original language, even though these classic works were written in the twelfth and thirteenth centuries.

Historians believe Iceland's physical isolation from foreign influences prevented its written language from changing. Icelandic pronunciation, however, has evolved over time. Icelandic scholars periodically remove from written works foreign words that have crept into everyday vocabulary. Language experts in the 1800s even created new words to replace Danish and German words that Icelanders had adopted.

Icelanders address one another by their first names, and few separate family names exist in the country. Last names consist of the father's first name plus "son" for boys or "dóttir" for girls. For example, if a man named Jón Einarsson has a son named Stefán and a daughter named Helga, Stefán becomes Stefán Jónsson and Helga becomes Helga Jónsdóttir. If Helga married, she normally would not take her husband's name but would be called Mrs. Jónsdóttir.

Literature

Iceland has a very strong literary tradition that dates to the country's founding. The first settlers told stories and recited poetry about characters and events that were part of their heritage from Scandinavia and the British Isles. Such tales formed the basis of the sagas—long works of fiction that described Iceland's early heroes and heroines.

The sagas detail the abilities and shortcomings of their characters. Among the sagas that have been translated into many languages are *Njal's Saga, Egil's Saga,* and *Laxdaela Saga.* The author of *Egil's Saga* is Snorri Sturluson, who was born in 1179. He also wrote a history of the kings of Norway and stirring tales of gods and heroes. During the 1200s, Icelandic scholars put together the *Poetic Edda.* Its long poems are based on heroic legends that originated in Germany and in other parts of Europe as early as the fifth century.

The sagas and early poetry have been a source of entertainment, education, and cultural pride for Icelanders for centuries. While Iceland was under foreign control,

however, the country's literature declined. One exception was Hallgrímur Pétursson's *Passion Hymns,* which he composed in the mid-1600s.

The independence movement that developed in Iceland in the nineteenth century inspired many poets. Jónas Hallgrímsson (1807–1845) wrote with great feeling about the natural features of his country. In the twentieth century, the island has produced many novelists and playwrights as well as poets. The writer Halldór Laxness enjoyed a wide following. His work earned him the Nobel Prize for literature in 1955. In his novels, short stories, plays, and poems,

An illustration from *The Saga of Gunnlaug and Hrafn* depicts the death of Helga. She was loved by Gunnlaug and Hrafn, two Icelandic warriors who fought over her until they both were killed. Helga loved only Gunnlaug and died clutching the expensive cloak he had given her.

Halldór wrote about Iceland's past and present in a style strongly influenced by the saga tradition.

The Arts

In the early twentieth century, Icelandic painters took their inspiration from their country's natural beauty, depicting it in many landscapes. Ásgrímur Jónsson, Jón Stefánsson, and Johannes Kjarval excelled in this style of painting. Since World War II, Icelanders such as Thorvaldur Skúlasson and Svavar Gudnasson have explored modern art.

Einar Jónsson pioneered modern sculpture in Iceland in the early 1900s. The Einar Jónsson Museum in Reykjavík displays many of his works. Another highly regarded sculptor from the same period is Asmundur Sveinsson, whose massive concrete creations appear throughout the capital. The modern artist Sigurjón Ólafsson opens his workshop and surrounding sculpture garden to the public.

For centuries, Icelandic artisans carved wood into decorative objects that graced churches and farmhouses. The national museum now displays many of these pieces, along with ancient tapestries. Some modern Icelandic artists use lava to create ceramic pieces that are famous for their sleek shape and simple style.

Singing and instrumental music, which have long been popular in Iceland, enjoyed a rebirth in the early 1800s. Icelandic composers frequently worked the country's folk tunes into their classical music. During the late nineteenth century, Sveinbjörn Sveinbjörnsson composed the melody for the Icelandic national anthem, using words by the poet Matthías Jochumsson.

Courtesy of Leonard Soroka

A streetside vendor offers warm Icelandic sweaters for sale. The heavy garments, which are made from the wool of locally raised sheep, are an established export item and provide ongoing employment to many Icelandic weavers.

A large statue by the Icelandic sculptor Asmundur Sveinsson represents a black bear.

Made of many small pieces of colored glass, this stained-glass window is an example of abstract art, which often is not meant to depict an object or person.

The National Museum in Reykjavík houses many early works by Icelandic craftspeople *(above).* **The chairs, cloth hangings, and chests date from the country's ancient times. Another Icelandic craft appears in the geometric patterns of wood and dirt, which were used to cement the walls of early dwellings** *(right).* **These materials helped to keep out cold air in winter, while in summer the homes remained pleasantly cool.**

Fireworks light up the sky over Reykjavík on New Year's Day.

Religion and Holidays

More than 90 percent of Iceland's people officially belong to the Evangelical Lutheran Church, the national church of Iceland. But most Icelanders do not regularly attend services. Headed by a bishop, Iceland's church is supported by a tax on all its members.

Laws have established freedom of religion. Other sects represented in Iceland in-clude the Roman Catholic Church, the Lutheran Free Church, and the Seventh-Day Adventists.

Most Christian holy days and a number of special holidays are observed in Iceland. Seamen's Day, in late May, is dedicated to Icelandic sailors and is celebrated with speeches, processions, rowing competitions, and lifesaving displays. Iceland's National Day is June 17, the date both of

Jón Sigurdsson's birth and of the establishment of the republic.

Because it is illegal to cut fir trees, at Christmastime Icelanders decorate the evergreens that they have planted on family graves. Each year in Reykjavík, a tall Christmas tree arrives as a gift of the Norwegian people, whose ancestors settled in Iceland more than 10 centuries ago. On Christmas Eve, family members exchange gifts and eat special foods. The day after Christmas, called Boxing Day, is also a holiday. New Year's Day is ushered in with bonfires and fireworks.

Sports and Recreation

A form of wrestling called *glíma* is Iceland's national sport. Dating to at least the

Photo by John R. Day

Rural Iceland contains many small, simple Lutheran churches, which draw believers to services on Sundays and on major Christian holidays.

Photo © Mats Wibe Lund

With its abundance of fast-flowing rivers, Iceland attracts dedicated fishermen. These anglers cast for salmon in the Laxa River, which lies in the southwestern part of the country.

1100s, the sport developed out of self-defense techniques. In glíma, two opponents grip each other's belts and use various wrestling techniques and foot movements to throw each other to the ground. Strict rules govern how the sport is played.

Football (soccer), skiing, and ice skating are popular sports, and basketball, handball, and golf also draw many participants. The country's many naturally heated pools allow Icelanders to swim year-round, even in the coldest weather. Windsurfers take advantage of the steady breezes in some of the country's protected bays. Chess and the card game bridge are favorite indoor activities, particularly during the dark winter months.

Both Icelanders and visitors enjoy angling for trout in crystal-clear lakes and fishing for salmon in well-stocked rivers. The Reykjavík marathon also attracts national and international runners, who enjoy competing in the pollution-free atmosphere. Held in the capital in August, the race is more than 26 miles long.

Food

Icelanders enjoy good food that is plentiful and attractively served. Meals that include dairy products, fish, and lamb are typical of Icelandic cuisine. Iceland's geography and climate limit the availability of locally produced beef, poultry, green vegetables, and fruits. These foods are not served as frequently as they are in other European countries.

Popular for the noon meal are open-faced sandwiches. They are made from single slices of thickly buttered bread topped with cheese, tomato, cucumber, sardines, or herring. The evening meal may be served either cold or hot. Typically, it begins with halibut or lamb accompanied by boiled potatoes. The meal usually ends with coffee and a dessert, such as *skyr,* a yogurt-like dish served with cream and sugar.

Special Icelandic delicacies include black caviar (fish eggs), smoked mutton, salted cod, and dried fish. Many Icelanders like boiled sheep's head or strong-smelling pickled shark. Shark that has been buried in sand for a long time is sometimes served as an appetizer.

Photo © 1991 Mats Wibe Lund

During celebrations for National Day, wrestlers compete in a *glíma* match. On their thighs and hips, the participants wear harnesses, which the wrestlers grab to throw their opponents to the ground.

Photo © 1991 Mats Wibe Lund

At Seydisfjördur in eastern Iceland, conveyor belts unload herring to waiting workers, who prepare the fish for export.

4) The Economy

Until the twentieth century, the people of Iceland depended on agriculture—especially the raising of livestock—for its survival. Farmers fished for food to help feed their families. Not until about 1900 did fishing replace agriculture as the mainstay of the Icelandic economy. Iceland is now an industrialized country, but most of its large business enterprises involve fishing and fish processing.

Fishing

In the mid-1990s, fish and fish products made up more than two-thirds of Iceland's exports. The Icelandic fishing fleet has more than 850 vessels, and the country claims fishing rights in waters up to 200 miles from the country's coasts. Iceland's trawlers also fish off the islands of Greenland and Newfoundland.

Herring, which are caught mainly in summer and fall, make up almost half of the yearly catch. Siglufjördur and other northern towns are centers of the herring industry. Local facilities preserve some herring through a salting process and turn the rest into oil and fish meal. Fishermen on the southwestern coast bring in cod—which are even more important than

Near Reykjavík, cod that have been slit lengthwise hang on wooden racks to dry. This age-old preservation method allows the fish to be shipped without refrigeration. Stockfish — an unsalted variety of dried fish — often ends up in countries with hot climates. Cooks soak the stockfish in water to return it to its pre-dried state and then add it to spicy vegetable stews.

herring to the national economy—in winter and early spring. Boats also return with ocean perch, catfish, halibut, plaice, sole, lobster, and shrimp.

In the 1930s, companies introduced methods of freezing fish quickly, and Icelandic fish processors built many plants where fish could be frozen for export. About 30 percent of Iceland's frozen cod fillets end up on dinner tables in the United States. Some fish are exported fresh, on ice, to Europe. Iceland also exports cod-liver oil, especially to Scandinavia, and trades fish with Russia for petroleum.

Because of its heavy dependence on fishing, Iceland is vulnerable to international events, such as wars and blockades, that might interfere with its ability to export fish. The country's income also is in jeopardy when overfishing depletes stocks in the North Atlantic Ocean. In the late 1980s, the ocean provided about 10 percent less cod than it had earlier in the decade. By 1990 the country was feeling the economic pinch of this drop.

At times, the entire hold of a boat may be full of freshly caught fish.

Most of the towns and villages on Iceland's northern fjords are entirely dependent on fishing and have no alternative sources of employment. People may have to abandon these small settlements if Iceland and other fishing nations do not limit hauls and carefully manage future supplies of fish.

Fishing vessels of all sizes use the ports that line the island's coasts. More than 100 different kinds of fish swim in Icelandic waters, but most are not valuable for export. The largest hauls are of herring, cod, perch, sole, and plaice.

Agriculture

Iceland's agricultural sector has always been based on raising livestock. Icelandic farmers mostly keep sheep and dairy cattle, along with a few hogs, goats, and beef cattle. The chief dairying region is in the south, near Selfoss. Sheep are the main source of meat in Iceland, and wool and sheepskins are important by-products. Poultry farms supply the country with chickens and eggs.

Planting grain is risky because of the country's short growing season. Grasses thrive, however, and hay for animal feed is the principal crop. Extended daylight in the summer and abundant rain allow many fields to yield three crops of hay each year.

Some farms grow vegetables, mainly potatoes, cabbages, turnips, beets, and onions. Greenhouses that operate on naturally heated water provide fruits and vegetables. Even cold-sensitive banana

Photo © 1991 Mats Wibe Lund

Marks on the horns or the ears of Icelandic sheep help owners to identify their herds at a roundup.

Because of its cold weather and short growing season, Iceland does not produce many fruits and vegetables outdoors. A variety of crops, however, thrive in greenhouses *(above)* that are heated with underground hot water. For example, tomato plants *(right)* flourish in the warm, sunny atmosphere of an indoor nursery. Staking the plants helps to increase their yield of ripe, unblemished fruit.

In the spring and autumn, farmers allow their sheep to graze on planted grasslands. In the summer, the herds go to communal pastures that cover the uplands and mountains. Icelandic sheep feed on preserved fodder called silage during the winter months.

trees can survive in Iceland's heated indoor nurseries.

An average farm has about 1,250 acres of land. Most farms use only a portion of their holding for pasturing livestock and for growing hay. In recent decades, many northern Icelandic families have abandoned their rural properties and have moved to villages to fish for a living. The land they left usually became part of a neighboring farm. With larger farms and improved agricultural methods, Icelanders who are still raising livestock are better able to succeed.

Photo by John R. Day

In summertime, when rainfall can be heavy in some regions, farmers often keep hay dry by wrapping it in white plastic bundles.

56

Manufacturing, Mining, and Trade

Manufacturing employs one-fifth of Iceland's total work force. Fish- and food-processing plants hire many of these workers. Also important in providing jobs are factories that produce consumer goods, such as shoes, clothing, furniture, soaps, paints, plastics, and appliances. In addition, the printing and publishing industries employ many people.

Iceland has very few mineral resources. Workers mine aluminum ore, pumice (volcanic stone), and Iceland spar (limestone and chalk) in small quantities. A facility near Mývatn brings up diatomite—a powdery substance used by industry as a filter and insulator—from the bottom of the lake. Iceland also has a cement factory at Akranes and a fertilizer plant near Reykjavík. These facilities meet the country's needs for those products.

Independent Picture Service

At a factory in Reykjavík, a worker fills bags with fertilizer, which is used locally rather than exported.

Photo © Mats Wibe Lund

The capital city has become the hub for industries that process fish and other foods.

A modern plant near Mývatn extracts diatomite, a powder that is needed to make filters and insulators.

Photo © Mats Wibe Lund

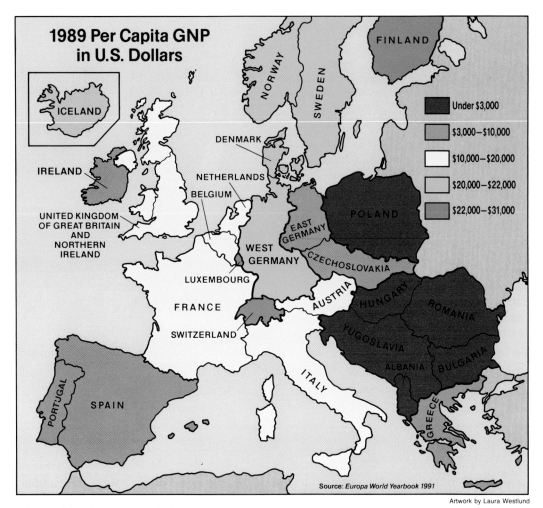

1989 Per Capita GNP in U.S. Dollars

■	Under $3,000
▨	$3,000–$10,000
□	$10,000–$20,000
▢	$20,000–$22,000
▨	$22,000–$31,000

Source: *Europa World Yearbook 1991*

Artwork by Laura Westlund

This chart shows the average productivity per person—calculated by gross national product (GNP) per capita—for 26 European countries in 1989. The GNP is the value of all goods and services produced by a country in a year. To arrive at the GNP per capita, each nation's total GNP is divided by its population. The resulting dollar amounts are one measure of the standard of living in each country. Iceland's 1992 figure of $17,000, combined with strong government welfare programs, still enabled Icelanders to live comfortable, healthy lives. The nation's recent economic hardships, however, have put this high standard of living at risk. (Data taken from *Europa World Yearbook, 1991*.)

An aluminum smelter began operating at Straumsvík in 1969 as a joint enterprise of the Icelandic government and a Swiss firm. The plant imports the raw material needed to make aluminum. This industrial site, the biggest in Iceland, is powered by a hydroelectric plant on the Thjórsá River.

Lacking raw materials and a large labor force, Iceland must import many of the nation's essential items. Major imports include machinery, ships, automobiles, pe-

troleum, metals, textiles, lumber, paper, and grains. The country gets most of these products from Great Britain, the United States, Germany, Russia, Norway, Sweden, and Japan.

Iceland is a member of the European Free Trade Association (EFTA). The nation also works with the countries in the European Union (EU). By a 1994 agreement, Iceland gained unlimited access to the huge EU market. In return, EU vessels were allowed to catch a limited number of fish in Icelandic waters.

Energy Sources

Iceland has an abundance of two clean, renewable energy sources. Geothermal energy comes from tapping the hot water close to the surface of the earth. The nation's many rivers also provide hydropower.

Reykjavík and other towns have built geothermal heating systems to carry hot water to the capital's houses and businesses. Pipelines direct the water where it

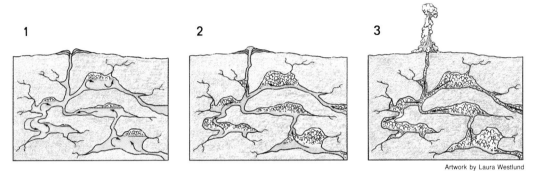

Artwork by Laura Westlund

Three diagrams show how geysers form. Groundwater creeps through the nooks and crannies in Iceland's hot, volcanic soil and rock (1). These materials heat the water, producing pressure and steam. The steam (2) forces the water upward toward a crevice that has an outlet at the surface. As the underground pressure builds, water and steam spurt through the opening as a geyser (3).

Courtesy of Iceland Tourist Board

Swimmers relax in a pool outside a geothermal plant. Icelanders can use some outdoor pools year-round because of the country's easy access to hot water.

Clouds of steam, called flashes, indicate where underground geothermal activity is taking place.

is needed. Ninety-nine percent of Reykjavík's residents rely on this service and pay very low heating bills.

The same hot-water supply fills many outdoor swimming pools so they can be used year-round. It also permits growers to raise vegetables, fruits, and flowers in greenhouses, providing fresh produce that would otherwise not be available to Icelanders.

At geothermal plants, hot water and steam are the energy sources that turn huge wheels called turbines. The turbines drive generators that produce electricity, which is sent to homes and businesses.

The fast-flowing rivers and high waterfalls of Iceland are also capable of supplying enormous amounts of hydroelectricity. Icelanders have just begun to use hydropower, which could provide an important export product in the twenty-first century.

Iceland imports all of its oil, mostly from Russia. Yet Iceland's dependence on foreign petroleum is lessening as more geothermal systems begin to operate. Each year increasing numbers of Icelanders hook up their homes to extensive hot-water pipelines that tap underground sources.

Transportation and Shipping

Until the early 1900s, Iceland had no roads, and travelers had to ride horses or use boats to get around. The government organized the first highway-building program in about 1900, and the introduction of the automobile in 1913 created a further demand for overland routes. By the early 1990s, Iceland had more than 7,500 miles of roads. Yet it is one of the few countries in the world with no railroads.

The island's rugged topography makes roads and bridges costly to build and maintain. Most highways are gravel surfaced with two lanes, but paved highways extend from Reykjavík to nearby towns. Workers completed a road around the entire island in 1974.

Trucks transport most domestic freight, and private companies run bus services throughout the country. Reykjavík and Akureyri have urban bus lines. Passengers and freight still move from town to town by boat. The country has 4 major and 50 minor ports. Coastal steamers take passengers from Reykjavík to all of the

Iceland's many short, rapidly flowing streams may be able to provide the country with vast sources of hydro-electricity.

Courtesy of John Rice

Iceland contains no railroads, and motorized traffic relies on the nation's road system. When rain or melted snow is heavy, paved routes become flooded, and vehicles have to wade through the water to continue their journey.

island's chief ports. In summer, regular ferry services are also available from eastern Iceland to the Faeroe Islands, to Norway, and to Scotland.

The State Shipping Service handles most coastal shipping, and several private companies and cooperatives deliver overseas shipments. Iceland has a large commercial fleet, with more than 80 ships crossing the oceans to foreign ports.

Iceland has about 100 usable airfields, 16 of which are large enough to handle commercial flights. International flights leave from and arrive at Keflavík Airport,

Fishing boats, passenger ferries, and cargo vessels crowd one of Iceland's many ports.

A volcano on Heimaey Island shoots fire and lava into the sky. Icelanders have long found ways to survive their country's climate and natural dangers.

A worker at a plant in Akranes prepares a fish fillet for freezing. Fish-processing jobs in Iceland may become harder to keep as stocks of seafood decrease in the North Atlantic Ocean.

and domestic air services are based at Reykjavík. The country has two international air carriers, Icelandair and the smaller Eagle Airlines.

The Future

In 1990 Iceland faced some serious economic problems. As fish supplies dropped, the future of fishing in the North Atlantic became uncertain. Rising unemployment in the fishing industry further endangered the country's high standard of living. Despite this situation, the country remains heavily dependent on fishing and related industries. In addition, natural disasters still threaten the lifestyles people have worked for generations to attain.

Yet, in this harsh land of volcanoes and glaciers, Icelanders have survived and prospered through hard work and a strong drive to succeed. These qualities have allowed the people to maintain a good lifestyle and make their future prospects look hopeful.

Index